The GARLIC BOOK

a garland of simple, savory, robust recipes

Susan Belsinger and Carolyn Dille

INTERWEAVE PRESS

The GARLIC BOOK

a garland of simple, savory, robust recipes ·

Susan Belsinger and Carolyn Dille

THE GARLIC BOOK
by Susan Belsinger and Carolyn Dille

Design, Susan Wasinger, Signorella Graphic Arts
Photography, Joe Coca, except as follows: pages 13, 18, and 24, Joanne Pavia; 21, Jerry Pavia
Photo styling, Linda Ligon
Production, Marc McCoy Owens
Photo accessories on page 57 courtesy of The Cupboard, Fort Collins, Colorado

Interweave Press, Inc.
201 East Fourth Street
Loveland, Colorado 80537
USA

printed in Hong Kong by Sing Cheong

Library of Congress Cataloging-in-Publication Data

Belsinger, Susan.
      The garlic book : a garland of simple, savory, robust recipes /
Susan Belsinger & Carolyn Dille.
            p.   cm.
      Includes bibliographical references and index.
      ISBN 0-934026-80-7 : $9.95
      1. Cookery (Garlic)   2. Garlic.   I. Dille, Carolyn.   II. Title.
TX 819.G3B45 1992
641.6'526--dc20   92-43730
                                                                  CIP

First printing: IWP—22M:293:CC

DEDICATION

This book is for our oldest and all intermediate ancestors,

who discovered, grew, and gave us garlic, and to the earth

who continues to sustain.

ACKNOWLEDGEMENTS

Even in a brief book long acknowledgements are due, though space is limited. To those closest to us, our families, friends, and colleagues, our deepest thanks. And to those farmers, writers, growers, and lovers of garlic, past and present, our widest thanks.

TABLE OF CONTENTS

Is garlic "as good as ten mothers", as the Telugu proverb of India says?* Its remarkably persistent champions throughout history have answered yes, contributing, variously, treatises on medicine or magic, recipes, celebrations, and fields of garlic to amplify the reasons why. Perhaps this love for an edible plant is irrational—but many rational people share it. Because we are among those for whom life without garlic would be unthinkable, we offer our reasons, gathered through years of cooking with and growing garlic, talking, reading, and learning about it, and generally falling under its curious spell.

"Ten mothers" is a strong simile, indicative of how garlic, more than any other plant, brings out the varied and opinionated nature of humankind. The olive, corn, bay laurel—to name a few others—each have long histories, devotees, sacred rites, even gods and goddesses, and restorative claims. But only garlic has earned a complete range of responses: from avid consumption to complete avoidance by individuals, social classes, and cultures; from old wives' tales to clinical studies; from silliness to divine honors. The grape has been similarly inspirational,

ONLY GARLIC HAS

EARNED A COMPLETE

RANGE OF RESPONSES:

FROM AVID

CONSUMPTION TO

COMPLETE AVOIDANCE.

This charming proverb also provides the title for a documentary film about garlic by California filmmaker Les Blank.

but only by virtue of its ability to intoxicate.

Some claim that garlic is intoxicating in the figurative sense; at the least, it is uncommonly stimulating to the senses of taste and smell. We've not found studies that describe how garlic acts on the pleasure centers of the brain, but indisputably it does so. We find it stimulating in the kitchen as well as at the table, whether we use a small amount to nuance a sauce or forty cloves to braise with lamb or chicken. Working with garlic—peeling, smashing, slicing, mincing it—gives us a feeling of pleasant anticipation that no other ingredient matches. Some cooks add it to every savory dish they make, whether the dish traditionally contains garlic or not. In many Mediterranean countries, the Middle East, Korea, Thailand, and the republics of the former Soviet Union, garlic is as indispensible as salt.

Stored garlic requires good ventilation; openwork baskets or net bags work well.

ATTITUDES AND ETIQUETTE

We have long suspected that garlic's noxious reputation is more in most peoples' minds than in their noses. Nevertheless, garlic lingers. Its strong and staying odor comes from diallyl disulfide, a compound which is activated by contact with oxygen. The compound is readily absorbed by the body, and is eliminated through the breath and the pores, announcing its presence to those nearby the person who has consumed it. The more garlic eaten and the more the

Whole heads of garlic, roasted with olive oil and sprigs of thyme, are a versatile and addictive condiment.

eater sweats, the stronger the garlic odor. Garlic consumed raw is stronger in flavor and odor than cooked garlic and seems to linger in the body longer. In one experiment, when cut garlic was simply rubbed on the soles of the feet and then washed off, the garlic odor was still exhaled by the lungs.

Antidotes to garlic breath have been recommended throughout the years, many of them including chlorophyll-rich plants, particularly parsley; in modern times, chlorophyll tablets are often substituted for the plants. Chewing caraway, cardamom, or fennel seeds has been a putative garlic odor neutralizer in various times and places. Because the odor of garlic is also exuded through the pores, these remedies have limited effectiveness, however.

In our experience, eating three or four sprigs of parsley after a garlicky meal does lessen the lingering taste and aroma in our own perception. However, studies, both formal and informal, have shown that garlic odor will out regardless of parsley or chlorophyll consumption. We eat garlic every day, usually in moderate amounts, and we believe that the body becomes adept at metabolizing the odor, and the nose accustomed to it. In Irma Goodrich Mazza's characteristically temperate view, "It would be hypocritical to pretend that in our house we always use garlic daintily and sparingly. Usually we are mindful of the other folks in the world and use it wisely. But now and then, circumstances permitting and the mood being mad, we cook a Saturday night dish and really enjoy it. Then we stay home the next day." We can report that though we do not always stay home, we have not yet suffered ostracism.

Contempt and Celebrations

Largely because of its odor, garlic has persistently been linked with the working classes. According to Pliny, the Egyptian Pharaohs gave garlic and onions in great quantity to the laborers who built the pyramids. Without modern status symbols for making class distinctions, such as Swiss watches and Italian racing cars, the elite in many societies made a taboo against eating garlic. Another taboo is associated with religion: in some schools of Christianity, Hin-duism, Islam, and Zen Buddhism, garlic's odor as it leaves the body is associated with the devil, unclean or evil spirits, and uncleanliness in general. In some religious contexts, garlic is thought to stimulate impure and unspiritual thoughts and desires.

These attitudes have been so common throughout history that writers from Aristophanes, Juvenal, and Horace to Shakespeare, Rabelais, and Cervantes traded on them in their works: characters who ate and smelled of garlic were invariably crude and low-class, with unbounded appetites. Still, close reading of some texts leaves open the possibility that the writers were actually ridiculing the prejudices of delicate and snobbish members of their audiences.

Beliefs and taboos notwithstanding, the taste for garlic remains undiminished in its strongholds in Provence, Egypt, China, Thailand, Korea, and the re-

IN HUNAN PROVINCE IN CHINA, SOME PEOPLE EAT MORE THAN 50 POUNDS OF ALLIUMS A YEAR. . . .

publics of Georgia, Ukraine, and Siberia. And it is increasing in the United States. The French have held garlic in high regard for cooking and medicine for centuries. A celebration of *aioli monstre* ("giant garlic mayonnaise"), served with fresh vegetables, bread, and red wine, is held every season in Provence, a tradition dating to the Middle Ages. The Egyptians and Chinese, too, have long and continuing records of garlic consumption. Citizens of Cairo celebrate the season's first green garlic in a kind of informal festival, eating it with other herbs and bread for a day or two. In Hunan province in China, some people eat more than 50 pounds of alliums a year, including garlic and such close family members as onions, scallions, and chives. Of the other regions mentioned, festivals may or may not be held, but consumption is prodigious; Korea and Thailand rank first and second among countries in garlic consumption.

Appreciation of garlic turns to revelry in northern California where the summer harvest festival at Gilroy, near the center of United States garlic production, draws thousands each year for feasting and fun, recipe contests, and the crowning of a garlic queen. Berkeley and Los Angeles hold garlic festivals featuring street food and special restaurant fare. In Berkeley, Chez Panisse restaurant and writer Lloyd John Harris, tireless garlic promoter who writes about his passion amusingly and informatively, combined to produce a Provençal-style celebration in 1976. Along with music and dancing, this event presented garlic in every dish on the menu, which changed daily.

MEDICINE AND MOTHERS

Garlic's written history, focusing primarily on its medicinal uses, is the largest and one of the oldest of any cultivated plant, being mentioned two, three, and four thousand years B.C. in Chinese, Greek, and Babylonian sources. The origin of the plant itself is lost in prehistory. Experts variously favor southwest Siberia, Syria, even Greece and Turkey, though the consensus centers on central and western Asia.

Garlic's reputation as a purifying herb has persisted throughout history; from bactericide (internal and external) to vermifuge, the list of ailments it claims to ameliorate or cure is long. Pliny lists sixty-one garlic remedies for problems ranging from madness to coughs to wild animal bites to low libido. He includes how to prepare the garlic (pounded, boiled, in honey, with wine or coriander); and mentions some inconvenient side effects (flatulence and thirst).

Ten mothers may not be too many for a plant that humans have esteemed for

Bundles of garlic fresh from the field create an earthy tapestry.

millenia as purifying, soothing, and strengthening. Researchers in the United States have found that babies show a preference for garlic-flavored mother's milk by drinking more and staying at the breast longer. Whether they, too, recognize this particular affinity between babies and garlic, Siberians, Ukrainians, and other western and central Asian peoples have long relied on garlic folk remedies to treat babies and children. Garlic milk, honey, or vapor is thought to be especially efficacious against coughs, colds, and whooping cough.

Western medicine has fitfully taken note of garlic's reputation during the past century—it was used as an antiseptic to treat wounded soldiers in World War I—but the first World Congress on the Health Significance of Garlic and Garlic Constituents didn't take place until 1990 in Washington, D.C. Fifty researchers from

around the world presented the results of their research on the role of garlic on cholesterol levels, stomach and skin cancer, and blood coagulation. Their experiments tested the responses of humans and laboratory animals to the treatment of garlic extracts and whole garlic as well as chives, scallions, and onions. During the past decade, researchers in Germany and other countries have found that garlic reduces LDL-cholesterol (the "bad" kind) and increases HDL - cholesterol (the "good" kind) by about 12 percent if eight or nine cloves, or their equivalent in garlic oil or pills, are taken daily. In fact, good news about garlic keeps coming from medical research, providing the kind of clinical evidence that Western doctors believe in.

Exactly how garlic bestows its health benefits is not yet clear, and still in question is whether some

beneficial elements are destroyed by heat or by the processing that renders garlic extracts odorless. Twentieth-century scientists are cautious about making claims, but it seems clear that including garlic in the daily diet contributes to good health. Some people are allergic to garlic, of course, and others complain of irritation or flatulence when they eat it, but for those who love to eat garlic, recent medicine reports are full of good cheer.

We do not have space to discuss all the past and present medicinal uses of garlic thoroughly. But without being able to chemically analyze allicin, diallyl disulfide, or any of garlic's seventy other active constituents, a lot of people over a long time have recognized its health-promoting properties: as good as ten mothers, or perhaps fifty physicians.

Garlic in the Kitchen

Cooks' Notes

Working with garlic is an earthy pleasure. Unwrapping the modest-looking bulb from its layers of protective covering recalls getting at other nuggets of goodness, such as pomegranate seeds or crab meat. Cutting cloves or rubbing them on toasted bread releases the odoriferous sulfur compounds, evoking immediate but ancient olfactory awareness. The sharpness and tingling aroma of raw garlic deepens, expands, or softens when garlic is heated.

Many people never acquire a taste for garlic because they have never tasted it in its natural state. Its processed forms—garlic salt, powder, and flakes—are acrid and distasteful even to garlic fans; chopped garlic preserved in oil is bitter with off-flavors; in addition, old garlic bulbs that are yellow, shriveled, moldy, or sprouting taste harsh, burning, or even rotten.

We are accustomed to thinking of garlic as a year-round staple, but it is a seasonal crop, and its flavor declines slowly after harvest. Like other edible members of the allium family— onions, leeks, and chives— garlic varies greatly in flavor according to where and how it is cultivated and to some extent, according to variety. Fortunately, the season is fairly long, and the U.S. crop is augmented by imported garlic. In California, where most of the nation's garlic is grown, mature bulbs of several cultivars of common garlic (*Allium sativum*) are harvested in July. Elephant garlic (*A. ampeloprasum*), a species

THE SHARPNESS AND TINGLING AROMA OF RAW GARLIC DEEPENS, EXPANDS, OR SOFTENS WHEN GARLIC IS HEATED.

professed garlic haters may like, is also harvested in mid-summer. Its flavor, mild and rather dull to our palates, virtually disappears in cooking, but the giant cloves, used raw, have a place in summer vegetable salads.

In early spring, usually late March and April, green garlic is available in some markets. Delicate and fresh in flavor like most young spring vegetables, it is harvested before the individual cloves form. It resembles a very long scallion, with a white tender bulb about 2 inches (5 cm) long, and a medium green-yellow stalk 14 to 18 inches (36 to 46 cm) long. Though the stalk is somewhat fibrous, most of it is usable if minced or sliced very fine. Green garlic may be substituted for the mature bulb; but as its flavor is mild, more of it will usually be needed. The thinly sliced tops make an attractive garnish for cooked foods and salads.

In April or May, many areas of the country receive the new harvest of garlic bulbs from Mexico. The outer skin of this variety is purple-ivory. The cloves have a good, fairly mild flavor, and are welcome as last season's U.S. crop becomes harsh-tasting and begins to dehydrate and sprout.

CUTTING AND STORING

Common garlic, though strong in flavor, is paradoxically a delicate ingredient, requiring care in handling and storage. Diallyl disulfide, distinctive to garlic, is oxidized by exposure to air and reacts with metal and acids, causing bitterness and harshness.

To retain its fine, nutty pungency, cut garlic by hand with a stainless steel knife, cleaver, or mezzaluna. Carbon knives may discolor garlic and give it a metallic flavor. Hand chopping results in small bits of garlic and releases only a small amount of

COMMON GARLIC,

THOUGH STRONG

IN FLAVOR, IS

PARADOXICALLY A

DELICATE INGREDIENT,

REQUIRING CARE IN

HANDLING AND STORAGE.

the pungent oil. On the other hand, a food processor chops unevenly and smashes the cloves, causing them to give up too much oil, which results in a harsher flavor. Similarly, an electric herb and spice grinder reduces garlic to a strong paste. These latter methods do have their place, as in preparing a marinade which will be brushed off later.

Use chopped garlic as soon as possible to minimize oxidation. If you are pressed for time, you may store chopped garlic covered with oil for as long as a day in the refrigerator. The flavor will not be as fine as just-chopped garlic, but will be acceptable.

A garlic press also releases a lot of oil. Pressed garlic is best in marinades or in stews and other cooked dishes which contain other strong flavors. A good way to decrease the oil—and make the press easy to clean—is to press the clove with the inner skin in place. Smashing gar-

Green garlic, harvested before the heads begin to form, is an early spring treat.

Glorious garden companions—parsley, tomatoes, garlic.

lic cloves, as Oriental cooks do, releases both the skins and some oil. Smashed garlic (with or without the skin attached) is usually cooked in oil to flavor it, then discarded. It also can be mashed thoroughly with an equal amount of salt, then rubbed on meat or poultry as a "dry" marinade. The salt helps keep the garlic from oxidizing.

When you need an entire head of garlic for a recipe, place it on a hard work surface and press the stem end with the heel of your hand. This requires a little strength, but the cloves will break apart cleanly under the pressure. Otherwise, just pull off cloves as you need them.

The inner skins of freshly harvested mature gar-

lic cling tightly to the cloves. This is a sign of good flavor, but it makes the cloves difficult to peel. Blanching does not help; it alters the flavor, and the garlic will not slip out nicely, as almonds do, because the skin is very firmly attached at the root end. There are two good ways to peel a tight-skinned clove: give it a quick whack with the flat of a knife or place the clove on a board, concave side down, and press it gently but firmly with your thumb. Either way, the skin will slip off easily.

Store mature heads and loose cloves out of direct sunlight in a cool place with plenty of air circulation. Dampness invites mold, so refrigeration is not recommended. Green garlic may be kept in a loose paper or plastic bag in a dry basement or in the refrigerator for a week or two. Stalks stored in the basement will dry a bit, but will still be usable for cooking. In the refrigerator, green garlic tends to impart a garlicky odor, especially to fruits.

We don't recommend canning garlic, partly for safety reasons (botulism has been found in commercial oil-packed garlic), and partly because it causes great changes in flavor. Freezing garlic also greatly alters its flavor and texture. The best way to keep garlic for extended periods is the one people have used for thousands of years: in its natural, whole-bulb form.

Cooking with Garlic

The taste of garlic can be strong or gentle, pungently hot or soothingly warm. Especially if you grow your own garlic, you can appreciate the differences in flavor, which vary according to season as well to cooking methods.

Frying brings out garlic's most common, pleasantly strong flavor. Use only medium or low heat, as garlic burns easily. Even if it is not burned brown or black, garlic can become quite acrid if cooked over high heat. In Singapore, Hong Kong, and parts of Indonesia, crispy fried garlic is much esteemed as a garnish (see page 41).

Poaching garlic (cooking it in a liquid over low heat) softens it and sweetens the flavor so that surprisingly large amounts may be used. Roasting the bulb produces a complex, nutty, caramelized flavor. If you like just a whisper of garlic in a milk- or cream-based sauce, try rubbing a wooden spoon—or the pan itself—with a cut clove, then stirring the sauce. Cooking garlic in an aluminum pot gives it a disagreeable flavor, especially when it is combined with acid ingredients such as tomatoes or lemons.

Rubbing a wooden salad bowl with garlic is not a good practice; the pungent oils will eventually turn rancid. To give a hint of garlic to salads, keep some garlic oil or vinegar on hand. These condiments are easily made by smashing the cloves and steeping them in either medium; the amount of garlic determines the strength of the flavor. We recommend making them in small amounts—no more than you will use in a month or two—because they can taste dull and musty when kept longer.

Garlic in the Garden

WHEN YOU'RE READY TO

PLANT, CHOOSE A SUNNY

LOCATION AND PREPARE

THE SOIL WELL.

Cultivation

Garlic is one of the easiest plants to grow in the home garden. By following the simple cultivation practices outlined below, you should harvest a goodly crop on your first try. The worst problem we have experienced is being beaten to the bulbs by gophers and moles.

One of the most important requirements is good drainage. Garlic is subject to fungal attacks in damp and poor-draining soil. Large-scale commercial growers have sometimes had to abandon garlic fields afflicted with soil-borne fungal diseases. If your garden soil is heavy, you may wish to construct a raised bed for your garlic.

Choosing healthy bulbs will also reduce the chances of fungal disease.

They should be firm and plump, not shriveled or discolored. Avoid any with soft spots or mildew. Bulbs can be bought at the grocery store or from a plant nursery, or mail-ordered.

In warm regions (hardiness zones 6 through 10), plant garlic in fall (September through November) as the bulbs need a long cool period in the ground to develop well. We recommend fall planting even in cold regions. Do this four to six weeks before the ground freezes, generally September and October, and cover the soil with ample mulch. Garlic can also be planted in early spring, but the bulbs will not be as large as those that have wintered over.

When you're ready to plant, choose a sunny location and prepare the soil well

Top-setting garlic, or rocambole, grows in interesting serpentine forms.

by working in organic matter such as compost or aged manure. Both sandy soils and heavy clay are improved by adding organic matter. If rice hulls are locally available, they are a good amendment to improve aeration and drainage in heavy clay soils.

Break your healthy and handsome heads of garlic into individual cloves, leaving the papery inner skins intact. Though many gardeners insist that garlic be planted with the pointed end up and the root end down, we like Stanley Crawford's thoughts from his beautifully written book, *A Garlic Testament*. In the chapter "Uprightness is All", he discusses the difficulties facing a garlic farmer who tries to hand-plant, root down, several thousand cloves of garlic: "That a plant that spends the greater part of the life cycle in the ground, a plant that survived millennia of global mismanagement by mankind, that such a plant

does not know at this late date which side is up?" In his experience, garlic rights itself by spring with the help of the shifts and settlings of soil and the pull of the sun.

Whether you just aim the cloves at furrows, or hand-set each one root down, plant them deep: 1 to 2 inches of soil covering the top of the cloves in hardiness zones 5 to 10, and as much as 4 inches in colder zones. In the herb or vegetable garden, plant the cloves 4 to 5 inches apart in rows about 10 inches apart to give them plenty of room to feed. Garlic is not out of place among flowers; the green tops can be as tall as 2½ feet, so place the cloves where you would like to see a slender vertical accent, such as in a border or as a background to small plants.

In the spring, fall-planted garlic sends up green shoots that become flat leaves. Flower stalks appear in late spring in some varieties; the flowers are edible,

and good in salads. Interspersed among the individual flowers are tiny bulbs called bulbils or bulblets. These should be harvested to encourage the growth of large bulbs; they are tasty and need not go to waste. Alternatively, they can be saved and planted; however, they will not produce harvestable garlic bulbs for at least two years.

The most important spring chore is weeding. Weeds can stifle a garlic patch, absorbing nutrients and light. Mulching helps to keep weeds down and the soil cool; though garlic tops need sun, the bulb grows best in cool soil. Spring is also the time to fertilize the garlic again for best bulb size. We've had good results with balanced (10-10-10 and 20-20-20) liquid fertilizers and manure tea. For the gardener, spring also brings the treat of green garlic, a delicacy found in few markets, from bulbs that were planted in the fall. Harvest the entire plant when the leaves are from 14 to 18 inches tall (36 to 46 cm) and before the individual cloves form.

Summer is when most of the bulb development takes place. Eventually the leafy tops wither. Once most of the tops fall and turn brown, harvest the bulbs. Dig the bulbs from dry soil rather than trying to pull the tops, especially if you would like to braid the garlic.

Garlic should be dried in a place with good air circulation, out of direct sunlight. We spread the heads with their foliage on old screens in a shed for a few days. Brush excess soil off the bulbs before braiding the tops, or remove the dried foliage from the bulbs before storing them in an open basket or mesh bag in a cool, dry place. Avoid dampness, which leads to molding and rotting of your crop.

VARIETIES

Allium sativum is the garlic commonly cultivated both commercially and in the home garden. Many varieties and cultivars exist. Some of the large, white-skinned types are referred to as American or Californian garlic; early and late cultivars are available. The many varieties with pink- or purple-skinned bulbs may be called Chilean, Creole, Mexican, or Italian. Garlic grows well all over the continental United States, although it does best in dry, mild regions. In the north, it does not develop as large a bulb because of the shorter growing season. Elephant garlic (*A. ampeloprasum*) is a garlic relative whose prodigious heads of four to six cloves can reach the size of an orange. Ours has grown only as large as lemons, but we are not too disappointed, as its flavor does not have the liveliness and interest of *A. sativum*.

"A PLANT THAT SURVIVED

MILLENNIA OF GLOBAL

MISMANAGEMENT BY

MANKIND, THAT SUCH A

PLANT DOES NOT KNOW

AT THIS LATE DATE WHICH

SIDE IS UP?"

—*Stanley Crawford*

Newly harvested mature garlic is at its peak of flavor.
Several varieties have attractive pink or purple skin.

Rocambole (*A. sativum* var. *ophioscorodon*), also called top-setting, serpent, Italian, or French garlic, is an allium we have seen in other gardens but have never grown ourselves. It looks rather dramatic, with many flat leaves like those of garlic chives (*A. tuberosum*) appearing in spring and looped flower stalks in summer. The "flower" head opens to reveal a cluster of bulbils instead of flowers. All parts of the plant are edible, and rocambole bulbs are harvested like those of *A. sativum*. According to those who have grown it, rocambole is well worth growing for several reasons: the bulbs keep well, the cloves peel easily, and the flavor is good. The bulbils may be planted like the cloves of common garlic, but will take two years to reach maturity. Rocambole is available by mail order but is seldom offered at nurseries.

APPETIZERS AND FIRST COURSES

Italian Garlic Bread

ITALIAN GARLIC BREAD

Fettunta is the Tuscan name for this crusty, whole wheat garlic bread. It can be toasted in the oven, but we like it best grilled over a wood fire. The toasted bread acts as a grater, releasing garlic oil and tasty bits of garlic onto the slightly rough surface.

12 slices country bread, 3/4 to 1 inch (about 2 cm) thick
About 1/2 cup (120 ml) extra-virgin olive oil

About 1/2 teaspoon (2 ml) salt
4 to 6 garlic cloves, peeled

Toast the bread until golden brown on both sides over an open flame or under the broiler. Mix olive oil and salt in a flat dish.

When the toast is cool enough to handle, firmly rub the garlic cloves over both sides for a strong garlic flavor or just one side for a milder one. Dip one side of each slice briefly in the oil and serve immediately.

AMERICAN GARLIC BREAD

1-pound loaf French or Italian bread
8 tablespoons (120 ml) unsalted butter, softened
3 or 4 garlic cloves, pressed
1/3 cup (80 ml) freshly grated parmesan cheese

2 teaspoons (10 ml) minced marjoram or oregano or 3/4 teaspoon (4 ml) dried marjoram or oregano

There are many styles of garlic bread and we have tried most of them. Our version of one served in many Italian-American restaurants uses Italian parmesan and herbs for a special touch.

Preheat the oven to 350°F (180°C).

Cut the loaf into 1/2 to 3/4 inch (1 to 2 cm) slices, leaving the bottom crust attached. Mash the butter and pressed garlic together, and blend in the cheese and herbs. Spread butter mixture on both sides of each slice, wrap loaf tightly in foil, and bake for 20 minutes. Serve hot.

Spaghetti con Aglio e Olio

1 pound (450 g) thin spaghetti or
  linguine
6 garlic cloves, minced
1/3 to 1/2 cup (80 to 120 ml)
  extra-virgin olive oil

Salt and freshly ground pepper
Freshly grated parmesan cheese,
  optional

This simple, famous dish is found in Italy on tables in farmhouses and in fine restaurants. Purists prepare it with just the finest durum pasta, freshest garlic, and extra-virgin olive oil. Others add hot pepper flakes and garnish it with minced Italian parsley and/or freshly grated parmesan. Whatever the variations may be, the basics remain the same: flavorful olive oil, fresh garlic, and al dente pasta.

Bring abundant water to a rolling boil. Salt it and stir in the spaghetti. Prepare the sauce while the pasta is cooking.

Heat the garlic in 1/3 cup (80 ml) oil in a frying pan over low heat. When the garlic just begins to bubble, stir and cook for 3 more minutes. Do not let it brown. Remove the pan from the heat.

When the pasta is al dente, drain it, add it to the frying pan, and toss it well. Season to taste with salt and pepper and add a bit more oil if you like.

Transfer the pasta to a warm platter or to individual bowls and serve immediately. Pass parmesan cheese if desired.

GARLIC SOUFFLÉ

Italian fontina gives this soufflé a nice consistency and flavor, but any melting cheese you like may be substituted. This dish is also good with the addition or substitution of green garlic or garlic chives.

4 tablespoons (60 ml) unsalted butter
3 tablespoons (45 ml) all-purpose flour
1½ cups (360 ml) milk at room temperature
1 head roasted garlic (page 65)
Salt and freshly ground pepper
5 egg yolks

4 ounces (115 g) Italian fontina cheese, cut into 1/4-inch (5-mm) dice
1/2 cup (120 ml) freshly grated Italian parmesan cheese
6 egg whites
Handful of garlic chives or green garlic, cut fine, optional

Melt 3 tablespoons (45 ml) of the butter in a heavy-bottomed saucepan over medium-low heat. Stir the flour in all at once and cook over low heat for 2 to 3 minutes. Add the milk all at once, stirring vigorously. Cook the mixture over low heat for about 15 minutes, stirring occasionally, to make a béchamel.

Meanwhile, press the roasted garlic from its skins to make a rough puree. Off the heat, salt and pepper the béchamel lightly and whisk in the roasted garlic. Cover and cool to room temperature.

Stir the egg yolks, the fontina, and all but 2 tablespoons (30 ml) of the parmesan into the cooled béchamel. Butter a shallow 10-inch gratin dish or pie plate thickly and dust it with the remaining parmesan cheese. Preheat the oven to 450°F (230°C).

Beat the egg whites until they are stiff but not dry. Stir a little of the beaten whites into the béchamel mixture, then fold in the rest in two parts. Fold in the optional green garlic or garlic chives.

Carefully pour the soufflé mixture into the prepared dish and bake for 18 to 20 minutes, until the soufflé is a rich golden brown on top but still creamy in the center. Serve immediately.

GARLIC SOUP

1 head of garlic
1½ quarts (1½ litres) chicken
    stock
4 ounces (115 g) stale country
    bread, 2 or 3 days old

Salt and freshly ground pepper
A few green garlic leaves, cut very
    thin, or shredded basil leaves,
    optional
Extra-virgin olive oil, optional

Peel the garlic and poach the cloves in 2 cups (475 ml) simmering broth. When garlic is completely soft, in 10 to 15 minutes, puree the mixture in a blender.

Meanwhile, trim the crust from the bread, and cut the remaining bread into cubes. Soak them in warm water until very soft, about 10 minutes, then squeeze out the excess water and crumble them.

Add the pureed garlic to the remaining broth, and whisk in the softened, crumbled bread. Salt and pepper the soup and simmer it for 10 minutes. Serve hot, garnished with garlic leaves or basil, and good olive oil drizzled in at the table, if desired.

Over the years we have experimented with garlic soups from French, Spanish, and Mexican cuisines, with mixed results. Some have turned out to be either insipid or harsh but not this version, which is finally satisfying: full of flavor but not overpowering. It is good before any Mediterranean, Southwestern, or Mexican main course. It also makes a fine peasant-style dinner, with a poached egg perhaps, or simply accompanied by some good bread, a salad, and a bit of cheese.

Tomato, Bread, and Garlic Soup

In Italy, this wholesome, peasant-style soup is called Pappa al Pomodoro. Its porridge-like consistency looks rather strange to Americans and depends a lot on the type of bread that is used. We like a simple country loaf that has a crunchy crust and a firm crumb. Whole wheat sourdough bread is a good alternative, but breads made with all white flour may tend to be gummy.

The soup can be served hot, cold, or at room temperature. We like it straight from the pot after it has sat for about an hour—just soothingly warm. Simple to make and delicious to eat, this dish can make a satisfying meal with a glass of red wine and a salad.

8 garlic cloves
1 small dried red chili pepper
3/4 cup (180 ml) extra-virgin olive oil
2½ pounds (1.1 kg) red ripe tomatoes, peeled and chopped
3 tablespoons (45 ml) shredded basil leaves
1 tablespoon (15 ml) shredded mint leaves
1/2 teaspoon (2 ml) salt
Freshly ground pepper
4 cups (1 litre) hot vegetable or chicken stock
1 pound (450 g) day- or two-day-old country whole wheat bread
Extra-virgin olive oil
Freshly grated parmesan cheese

Pound the peeled garlic cloves and the dried chili in a mortar and pestle until they are well crushed. Heat the olive oil in a large noncorrodible sauté pan or soup pot over low heat. Add the garlic and chili and soften over low heat for about 3 or 4 minutes.

Add the tomatoes, basil, and mint and stir and cook over medium-low heat for about 5 minutes. Add salt and pepper to taste and cook for another minute or two. Add the stock and bring to a boil.

While the stock is heating, cut the bread into 3/4-inch (2-cm) cubes or tear it into bite-sized pieces. When the stock comes to a boil, add the bread all at once. Stir well over medium heat until all the bread is moistened with the liquid.

Cover the pan and remove it from the heat. Let the soup stand for about an hour before serving. Taste the soup for seasoning and stir well. Serve the soup in bowls drizzled with a little olive oil. Garnish with freshly grated parmesan.

Tomato, Bread, and Garlic Soup

White Pizza

White pizza offers garlic and pizza lovers several variations: choose fresh, minced garlic or use roasted garlic; add fresh mozzarella, American-style mozzarella, or Italian fontina; sprinkle with your choice of chopped fresh oregano, rosemary, or sage. Any version is a fine first course before simple meals.

Pizza Dough

This recipe yields enough dough for the following quantities of pizza:
6 pizzette, each about 6 inches (15 cm) in diameter
4 pizzas, each about 9 inches (23 cm) in diameter
2 pizzas, each about 12 inches (about 30 cm) in diameter

2 teaspoons (10 ml) active dry yeast
1½ cups (360 ml) water
3½ cups (830 ml) unbleached white flour
1/2 cup (120 ml) whole wheat flour, or use another 1/2 cup (120 ml) white flour
2 tablespoons (30 ml) olive oil
1 teaspoon (5 ml) salt

Dissolve the yeast in about 1/4 cup (60 ml) water which is quite warm. When the yeast has become foamy, in about 10 minutes, add it to the rest of the water, which should be lukewarm.

Mix the flours and make a well in the center. Gradually stir the water and yeast into the well. Add the olive oil and salt. Gather the dough and knead it for 7 or 8 minutes, or until it is soft and lively.

Let the dough double in bulk in a lightly oiled bowl, preferably in the refrigerator overnight. Punch the dough down, divide it into portions, and roll these lightly into balls. Let them rest, covered with a towel, on a lightly floured surface for 20 minutes, or until the dough comes to room temperature if it was refrigerated.

Stretch the dough gently with your hands on lightly oiled baking pans, or on floured bakers' peels if you will be baking it on a baking stone. Let the dough rise in a warm place, covered, for 15 minutes before topping or filling and baking.

Preheat the oven and baking stone for 30 minutes at 500°F (260°C), or preheat the oven for 15 minutes at 450°F (230°C) if you are baking on metal pans.

Pizza dough can be frozen in pizza-sized balls after it has risen and been punched down. Thaw and let rise again before proceeding.

Topping

6 garlic cloves, peeled and minced, or
    8 roasted garlic cloves (page 65)
3 tablespoons (45 ml) olive oil
Salt

8 ounces (225 g) grated or diced
    fresh mozzarella, whole-milk
    mozzarella, or Italian fontina
    cheese, or a mixture
2 or 3 sprigs fresh oregano, rosemary,
    or sage, optional

Mix the garlic with the olive oil, mashing the roasted cloves well into the oil. Spread this mixture on the prepared pizza dough. Season lightly with salt.

Scatter the cheese evenly over the pizzas except on the rims.

Bake the pizzas until they are done, from 7 or 8 minutes to 15 minutes, depending on whether you are using a baking stone or metal baking pans.

For an herb garnish, chop the leaves and sprinkle them over the pizzas before cutting and serving.

SPICY GRILLED SHRIMP

During the years we owned a catering business between Baltimore and Washington, D.C., this was one of our most popular dishes. Because of our experience there, we are reluctant to say how many the recipe serves. We could put it this way: six to eight ordinary people, three or four shrimp lovers, or one or two Congressional aides. For an attractive presentation, shell the shrimp leaving the tail shell intact.

2 pounds (900 g) medium shrimp (26–30 count), preferably fresh
5 or 6 large garlic cloves
1/3 cup (80 ml) extra-virgin olive oil
1/4 cup (60 ml) fresh lemon juice
1/2 teaspoon (2 ml) hot red pepper flakes, or to taste
Salt

Shell and devein the shrimp, rinsing only if necessary. Mince the garlic. Place the shrimp in a shallow dish just large enough to hold them in one layer, and toss them with the minced garlic, olive oil, lemon juice, and red pepper flakes. Marinate the shrimp covered in the refrigerator for several hours or overnight.

Remove the shrimp from the refrigerator 30 minutes or so before cooking them. If you are grilling the shrimp over charcoal, have the coals medium hot. If you are broiling the shrimp in the oven, preheat the broiler.

Salt the shrimp lightly, then grill or broil them about 6 inches (15 cm) from the heat source for about 1½ minutes on each side. Serve the shrimp hot on a warm platter.

SAUCES

Agliata: Ligurian Bread and Garlic Sauce

Agliata: Ligurian Bread and Garlic Sauce

Makes about 2 cups (475 ml)

The Italians, especially the Tuscans and Ligurians, are very fond of bread crumb sauces. They serve them with poached meats, poultry, and fish, with simple roasts, and with floured and fried fish, brains, or sweetbreads. Since discovering these sauces while living in Italy, we must confess we eat them with almost anything, even on bread! Agliata is good with grilled eggplant; boiled, grilled, or baked potatoes; steamed artichokes; and thick slices of summer-ripe tomatoes. For variety, add some finely chopped basil, a handful of pine nuts or walnuts, and a small peeled and seeded tomato.

About 1/2 pound (225 g) or 1/2 loaf day- or two-day-old country bread, crust removed
1/4 cup (60 ml) red wine vinegar
1/4 cup (60 ml) water
4 garlic cloves
6 to 8 sprigs Italian parsley
About 3/4 cup (180 ml) extra-virgin olive oil
Salt and freshly ground black pepper

Cut the bread into small cubes or make rough crumbs in a food processor and soak these in the vinegar and water for about 15 minutes. Meanwhile, mince the garlic, and chop the parsley leaves. Squeeze the bread as dry as possible.

Pound the bread and garlic to a paste in a mortar and pestle, or combine them carefully in a food processor. Do not over-process. Stir in the chopped parsley.

If you are using a mortar and pestle, add the oil as for mayonnaise, a few drops at a time, increasing the amount of oil as the sauce begins to emulsify. If you are using a food processor, add the oil all at once and just pulse to mix.

Season to taste with salt and pepper. The sauce will not absorb the oil completely. The thin film of oil on top is traditional, but you may stir it into the agliata before serving.

GARLIC MAYONNAISES

Aioli

4 or 5 garlic cloves
1 egg yolk
3/4 cup (180 ml) olive oil

About 1 tablespoon (15 ml) lemon juice
Salt and freshly ground pepper

Slice the garlic very thin and pound the slices to a paste in a porcelain or marble mortar and pestle. (Some small bits will not completely break down.) If you don't have a mortar and pestle, mince the garlic very fine, then mash it well with the flat of a cleaver or large knife.

Stir the egg yolk into the garlic paste and then stir in the lemon juice. Add the oil drop by drop at first, stirring constantly. After you have added about 1/4 cup (60 ml), drizzle in the rest in a thin stream, stirring constantly until the mayonnaise has emulsified. Season with salt and pepper, adding more lemon juice, if desired.

To make the mayonnaise in a food processor, place the garlic paste, egg yolk, and lemon juice in the processor, then drizzle the oil through the feed tube in a thin stream until the mayonnaise emulsifies. Season with salt, pepper, and lemon juice.

Refrigerate the mayonnaise in a tightly covered glass jar for as long as a week. The flavor is best when the mayonnaise is fresh, but any left over is good in salads.

The most famous garlic mayonnaise is the Aioli of Provence, but commercial mayonnaise can be used as a base for a very decent garlic mayonnaise, and green garlic mayonnaise is a special treat when you can harvest your own green garlic stalks or find them in the market. Any of the versions given here may be used in place of ordinary mayonnaise in any dish, but they are exceptional as dipping sauces for crisp-tender asparagus, carrots, cauliflower, steamed or grilled artichokes, and raw radishes, celery, and fennel.

Garlic mayonnaises are good garnishes for cold steamed mussels, scallops, and shrimp and for grilled vegetables, meat, poultry, and fish. One of our favorite variations is to crush five or six fresh basil leaves with the garlic.

Green Garlic Mayonnaise

2 green garlic stalks	About 1 tablespoon (15 ml) lemon
1 egg yolk	juice
3/4 cup (180 ml) olive oil	Salt and freshly ground pepper

Trim the root ends from the garlic. Trim the stalks to about 9 inches (23 cm) long and remove the outer layer. Slice the garlic very thin.

Proceed as for Aioli, above.

Quick Garlic Mayonnaise

2 or 3 garlic cloves	2 tablespoons (30 ml) olive oil
3/4 cup (180 ml) commercial	2 teaspoons (10 ml) lemon juice, or
mayonnaise	to taste

Slice the garlic and reduce it to a paste as described above, then whisk it into the mayonnaise. Add the olive oil in a fine stream, whisking continuously. Finally, whisk in the lemon juice.

Green Garlic Mayonnaise and Aioli

Yogurt, Garlic, and Herb Sauce

Makes about 2 cups (475 g)

This quick sauce is our take on the yogurt sauces of Middle Eastern cookery. We like it with vegetable pies such as coulibiac, steamed or grilled vegetables, and grilled meat, fish, and chicken.

2 or 3 garlic cloves
Salt and freshly ground pepper
1 cup (240 ml) unflavored yogurt
1/2 cup (120 ml) sour cream

1/3 to 1/2 cup (80 to 120 ml) chopped mixed herbs: dill, chervil or tarragon, and parsley

Pound the peeled garlic cloves in a mortar and pestle, or mince and then mash them well with the flat of a cleaver or large knife. Place the mashed garlic in a bowl, salt and pepper lightly, then stir in the yogurt, sour cream, and mixed herbs, blending well.

Cover and let stand at cool room temperature or refrigerate for at least 2 hours. Adjust the seasoning before serving and serve at cool room temperature.

Makes about 2 ½ cups (600 ml),
enough for 8 servings of pasta

6 garlic cloves, sliced thin
1/3 cup (80 ml) pine nuts
2 cups (475 ml) packed basil leaves

3/4 cup (180 ml) freshly grated
Italian parmesan cheese
1/2 cup (120 ml) olive oil

If you make the pesto in a mortar and pestle, pound the garlic first, then the pine nuts. Chop the basil and add it by the handful, pounding it in well. Stir in the cheese and oil alternately, a little at a time.

If you use a food processor or blender, place all the ingredients in the container and pulse the motor to make a homogeneous sauce which is not as fine as a puree.

For centuries, Italians have come up with variations of pesto, keeping the basic trinity of fresh basil, fresh garlic, and good olive oil intact but changing the kinds of cheese and nuts, and often adding parsley. This classic version has that sharp, clean, strong freshness on the palate that makes pesto so attractive.

Serve pesto with pasta or as a dip with raw or cooked vegetables, and add it to minestrone or other vegetable soups.

CREAMY GARLIC AND MUSHROOM SAUCE

Makes sauce for 1 pound (450 g) pasta,
about 4 servings

This sauce, flavored with a hint of marsala, is delicious served over fresh fettuccine or cheese-filled pasta. Porcini lend a richer flavor to the sauce, but shiitakes are good, too. If you use shiitakes, be sure to remove the tough stems after the mushrooms have soaked.

1/2 ounce (15 g) dried porcini or shiitake mushrooms
1 cup (240 ml) boiling water
6 garlic cloves, minced
3 tablespoons (45 ml) unsalted butter
8 ounces (225 g) domestic mushrooms, sliced thin
3 tablespoons (45 ml) marsala

1 cup (240 ml) whipping cream (double cream)
1/2 teaspoon (2 ml) minced thyme or a scant 1/4 teaspoon (1 ml) dried thyme leaves
Salt and freshly ground pepper
1/2 cup (120 ml) freshly grated parmesan cheese plus more for garnish
Flat-leaved parsley, chopped

Pour boiling water over the dried mushrooms in a glass bowl and let soak for about 30 minutes. Strain the liquid from the mushrooms and reserve; there should be between 2/3 and 3/4 cup (160 to 180 ml). Rinse the mushrooms if they are gritty. Slice or tear them into bite-sized pieces.

Soften the garlic in the butter in a sauté pan over very low heat for 3 to 4 minutes. Do not brown. Add both sliced and soaked mushrooms and cook for about 3 minutes, stirring occasionally. Add the reserved stock and the marsala and simmer for about 3 minutes.

Add the cream, thyme, and salt and pepper to taste. Cook the sauce over medium heat, stirring occasionally, for about 10 minutes. It should be reducing slowly.

Add the parmesan and cook for about 5 minutes longer. Taste for seasoning; toss it with pasta cooked al dente, and serve hot, garnished with parsley and additional parmesan.

MAIN COURSES

Chicken with 40 Cloves of Garlic

Chicken with 40 Cloves of Garlic

Serves 4 to 6

Exact number of cloves is not as important as the idea—lots of garlic—in this old farmhouse dish claimed by most provinces of southern France. The important technique here is to be sure the casserole is completely sealed so that no condensed cooking juices escape. Most original recipes call for sealing vessel and lid together with a flour and water paste. We find that covering a pan with foil before fitting the lid works well. The dish can be cooked in a slow, 250°F (120°C) oven, or braised over low heat, as we usually do. A nice variation is to use white wine instead of the chicken broth.

3- to 4-pound (about 1.5 kg) chicken
Salt and pepper
3 tablespoons (45 ml) olive oil
40 garlic cloves: 3 or 4 heads of garlic

3 parsley sprigs
1 thyme or tarragon sprig
1/2 cup (120 ml) chicken broth
Country bread, toasted

Cut the chicken into serving pieces or have the butcher do this. Rinse them well, pat dry, and season lightly with salt and pepper.

In a large noncorrodible casserole with a tight-fitting lid, heat the oil and brown the chicken in it. When the chicken is browned all over, drain the fat from the pan.

Add the garlic, parsley, thyme or tarragon, and broth.

Whether to peel the cloves or not depends on the time of year and your preference. We like to leave them unpeeled, but if you're using winter storage garlic, it is wisest to peel them to be sure the cloves are firm and healthy with no bruises, which even long cooking will not modify to sweetness. Cover the pan with foil, then place the lid firmly on top. Cook over very low heat for 2 hours. The chicken and garlic should be completely tender. Serve over toasted country bread.

GREEK-STYLE ROAST LAMB WITH GARLIC & OREGANO

1 leg of lamb, 5 to 6 pounds (about 2.5 kg)

4 to 6 garlic cloves

Salt and freshly ground pepper

2 teaspoons (10 ml) minced oregano or 1 teaspoon (5 ml) dried oregano

1 lemon

Remove excess fat from the lamb or have the butcher do this.

Peel the garlic cloves and crush them to a paste with about 1/4 teaspoon (1 ml) salt. Stir in the oregano.

Preheat the oven to 425°F (220°C).

Cut small, deep slits all over the lamb and push the garlic paste into them. Season the meat lightly with salt and pepper, rub it well with the cut lemon, squeezing out the juice, and place it in a roasting pan or baking dish.

Cook the roast for about 15 minutes, then reduce heat to 350°F (180°C). After 45 minutes, remove the fat from the pan and add 1 cup (240 ml) water or white wine. Continue cooking about an hour longer until the lamb is medium-rare to medium, or 130°F (54°C) internal temperature.

Let the roast stand 15 minutes before carving. Meanwhile, remove any fat from the roasting pan and reduce the pan juices or dilute them with a little water as necessary. Carve the roast in thin slices and serve it on a platter with or without potatoes. Pass the pan juices in a sauce dish.

Potatoes, quartered or sliced thick, can be added during the last hour of cooking for a homey dish that will make meat-and-potato people very happy. Garlic lovers will want to use the larger amount of garlic. Common or Italian oregano is good, but Greek oregano, rigani, gives an authentic touch.

KEBABS WITH MIDDLE EASTERN TOMATO SAUCE

This kind of spiced tomato sauce is served with rice or barbecued meats in the Gulf states. As the sauce will keep, covered, in the refrigerator for as long as ten days, it is worth making a double batch to try in different contexts. It's good with grilled sweet peppers and mushrooms, and makes a fine barbecued sparerib sauce. We like to simmer meatballs or small cultivated mushrooms in it to serve as appetizers.

Tomato Sauce
Makes about 2½ cups (600 ml)

1 tablespoon (15 ml) olive or vegetable oil

6 to 8 garlic cloves, sliced

2 pounds (900 g) vine-ripe tomatoes, peeled, seeded, and diced

1 teaspoon (5 ml) freshly ground pepper

1/2 teaspoon (2 ml) each toasted, ground cumin seed, paprika, and salt

1/4 teaspoon (1 ml) each toasted, ground coriander seed, cinnamon, and nutmeg

1/8 teaspoon (0.5 ml) each cayenne and ground cloves

Heat the oil over medium heat. Add the garlic and cook until it just begins to sizzle. Add the tomatoes, cover, and simmer 15 minutes.

Add the spices and simmer uncovered for 15 to 20 minutes, stirring occasionally, until the sauce is medium thick. Season with salt and pepper.

Kebabs

2 pounds (900 g) lamb or beef, well trimmed

About 2 tablespoons (30 ml) olive oil

4 garlic cloves, smashed

3 whole cloves, smashed

1 large sweet onion, such as Vidalia

Salt and freshly ground pepper

Cut the meat in 1-inch (2 cm) cubes, rub them with just enough oil to coat, and marinate them, tightly covered, with the garlic and cloves, for several hours or overnight in the refrigerator.

When ready to cook the kebabs, prepare a medium-hot wood or wood charcoal fire. Quarter the onion and separate the layers. Remove the meat cubes from the marinade and thread them on skewers alternately with onion pieces. Salt and pepper lightly.

Place the skewers on a rack 5 or 6 inches (12 to 15 cm) above the coals. Turn the kebabs once or twice and cook until the meat is medium rare, about 10 minutes.

Meanwhile, reheat the sauce over low heat.

To serve, arrange the kebabs on a bed of rice and pour the sauce over them.

SINGAPORE-STYLE FRIED NOODLES

This is an excellent one-dish meal, needing nothing else to be nutritionally sound and to please the palate with complex flavors. The recipe is adaptable—add leftover cooked chicken, pork, or vegetables; leave out the omelet garnish; experiment with Chinese cabbage, bok choy, or broccoli—but do fry the garlic garnish for an authentic Singapore touch.

2 eggs
Salt and freshly ground black pepper
3 or 4 green onions
1 to 3 fresh small hot red or green
   chilis, according to taste

Garnishes

6 large garlic cloves
About a tablespoon (15 ml) of oil
   for frying the eggs and garlic
6 or 8 coriander sprigs, leaves and
   stalks chopped

Prepare the garnishes first, as long as a few hours ahead.

Beat the eggs with salt and pepper and about a tablespoon (15 ml) of water. Lightly oil a frying pan, or cook the omelets without oil in a non-stick pan. Pour half of the egg mixture in the heated omelet pan over medium heat and cook it until set on one side, about 30 seconds.

Turn the omelet and cook the other side until done, about 30 seconds longer. Place the omelet on a plate and cook the other omelet.

Cool the omelets to room temperature, then roll them and cut them in thin strips.

Trim the green onions, leaving about 4 inches (10 cm) of green. Cut them diagonally into pieces about 1 inch (2 cm) long. Seed the chilis, then cut them in thin slices.

Mince the garlic and rinse it under cold water, then squeeze it very dry in paper towels. Heat about 1/2 tablespoon (8 ml) oil in a small sauté pan over medium-low heat. Add the garlic and reduce the heat to low. Cook the garlic, stirring occasionally until pale golden and crisp, about 4 minutes. Cool and crumble.

Noodles

14 to 16 ounces (400 to 450 g) fresh Chinese or Japanese wheat noodles

1/2 pound (225 g) small fresh shrimp or bay scallops

1/4 pound (115 g) fresh bean sprouts

2 garlic cloves, minced

2 tablespoons (30 ml) peanut or vegetable oil

1 tablespoon (15 ml) dark sesame oil

1 tablespoon (15 ml) dark soy sauce or sweet soy sauce

1/4 cup (60 ml) chicken broth or water

2 celery stalks, cut thin

Cook the noodles in ample boiling lightly salted water for 4 to 6 minutes. When done, drain and immediately rinse well with cold water. Noodles may be prepared a day ahead and refrigerated. Bring to room temperature before frying.

Shell and devein the shrimp, or trim the scallops of any cartilage. Rinse the bean sprouts under hot water to minimize their raw potato flavor and pinch off the seed "tails" if desired.

When ready to serve, heat a wok over medium heat, then add the peanut oil. Add the garlic and stir constantly until it just begins to color, about 10 seconds.

Add the shrimp or scallops, increase heat, and cook for 2 minutes. Add the sesame oil, soy sauce, broth or water, sliced celery, and parcooked noodles, toss well, and cook for about 2 minutes. If you are using cooked leftovers, add them at this time.

Add the bean sprouts and toss the the noodle mixture well for about a minute. Transfer the noodles to a warm serving platter and sprinkle the prepared garnishes over them, ending with the crisp garlic on top.

ITALIAN-STYLE MARINATED FISH

Serves 6 to 8

Most regions of Italy have at least one version of this very old dish. For centuries before refrigeration, it was a palatable way to extend the edibility of fresh fish. The inclusion of saffron in this recipe points to the region of Abruzzi, where some saffron is still harvested. The fish is especially nice in the summer as a first or main course preceding or following a starchy and/or creamy dish such as risotto or baked pasta.

1½ to 2 pounds (about 700 to 900 g) firm-fleshed white fish fillets about 1/2 inch (1 cm) thick. Choose from sea bass, halibut, cod, rock cod, or monkfish
Salt and freshly ground pepper
Flour
1/4 cup (60 ml) extra-virgin olive oil, plus more for garnish
1 cup (240 ml) dry white wine
1/3 cup (80 ml) white wine vinegar
1/2 teaspoon (2 ml) saffron threads
4 garlic cloves, smashed
4 to 6 Italian parsley sprigs
Country bread

Season the fish with salt and pepper and dredge it with flour. Heat the olive oil over medium heat until it just begins to shimmer. Fry the fish until it is just done, about 3 minutes on each side.

Remove the fish to a serving dish which will hold it in one layer. Add the garlic cloves and salt and pepper lightly. Simmer the wine with the vinegar and saffron in a noncorrodible pan over medium heat for about 5 minutes. Pour the wine mixture over the fish.

Cool to room temperature. Marinate the dish, covered, for at least 1½ hours in the refrigerator, turning the fish carefully once. Or, as is traditional, marinate it for a day or two.

Just before serving, stem the parsley, chop the leaves, and sprinkle them over the fish. Serve the fish in shallow bowls with some of the marinade for each portion. Pass olive oil to garnish and bread to accompany.

VEGETABLES AND SALADS

Wild Mushrooms with Garlic

WILD MUSHROOMS WITH GARLIC

Serves 4 to 6

The first time we were presented with plate-sized porcini, studded with tiny slivers of garlic, glistening with olive oil, and hot from a wood oven in Tuscany, we exclaimed in our beginning Italian, "Che profumo!" Aroma is the sensory sign that mushrooms and garlic together unfailingly offer agreeable eating. In spring and fall, true wild mushrooms are sometimes available in markets. Many specialty grocery stores carry cultivated oyster and shiitake mushrooms all year round, and they are very tasty in this simple preparation. The dish can be served as a vegetable accompaniment, with toast as a first course, or over ribbon noodles.

1 pound (450 g) wild or cultivated mushrooms such as porcini, chanterelles, morels, shiitake, or oyster mushrooms
2 or 3 garlic cloves, minced

3 tablespoons (45 ml) extra-virgin olive oil
Salt and freshly ground pepper
Chopped parsley, optional

Clean the mushrooms and trim the stems. Depending on their size, leave the mushrooms whole, or cut them in large pieces. Oyster mushrooms are best left whole, as they are very tender.

Heat the garlic with the oil in a sauté pan over medium heat. When the garlic just begins to sizzle, add the mushrooms and cook them, tossing frequently, until they are just done, 2 to 3 minutes. Season with salt and pepper and toss with parsley, if desired. Serve hot.

ROASTED GARLIC AND MASHED POTATOES

2½ to 3 pounds (1.1 to 1.4 kg)
  Idaho potatoes
1 head garlic, roasted in cloves
  (page 65)

About 1/4 cup (60 ml) milk, heavy
  cream, or half-and-half (single
  cream), optional
Salt and freshly ground pepper

Peel the potatoes, cut them into chunks, and simmer them in lightly salted water until they are just tender, about 15 minutes.

Drain the potatoes, reserving the cooking water. Squeeze the garlic cloves from their skins into the potatoes. Rice or mash the potatoes and garlic together with a potato masher or a fork. Do not use a food processor.

Return the mashed potatoes to the pan off the heat. Add 2 or 3 tablespoons (30 to 45 ml) of the flavored oil and about 1/3 cup (80 ml) of the cooking water. Add milk, cream, or more cooking water to obtain the consistency of mashed potatoes that you like. Season the potatoes and heat through.

Potatoes and garlic have a special affinity; this dish is an easy and delicious variation of mashed potatoes. Roasted garlic is also good spread on toasted or grilled bread, added to cheese soufflés, or used as a sauce for roasted or grilled chicken or grilled vegetables. For spreading on bread and adding to a soufflé base, squeeze the roasted cloves into a small bowl, add a little of the flavored oil in which they were roasted, and mash everything together well. For use as a sauce, add a few drops of wine vinegar.

Wilted Greens and Garlic

Use any of your favorite greens in this dish: spinach, chard, kale, beet, collard, dandelion, even a bit of arugula. These are good served as an accompaniment to roast meats or poultry. We also like to toss the greens with pasta, then sprinkle with pecorino cheese, or spread them on pizza and top with fresh mozzarella or a blend of mozzarella and pecorino.

1½ pounds (675 g) greens; a nice combination is 1/2 (225 g) pound each of spinach, collards, and kale

3 tablespoons (45 ml) olive oil
5 garlic cloves
Salt and freshly ground black pepper

Wash and pick over the greens and remove tough stems. Put the leaves with the water that clings to them in a large noncorrodible pot with a tight-fitting lid. Wilt them over medium-high heat for about 5 minutes, stirring once or twice, adding a bit more water if necessary. The leaves should be just wilted.

In a large sauté pan, gently heat the olive oil over medium-low heat. Crush the garlic through a press or mince it and add it to the pan. Gently sauté the garlic for 2 or 3 minutes; do not allow it to brown.

Drain the greens and add them to the sauté pan. Cover and cook over medium heat for 6 to 8 minutes, stirring occasionally.

Season with salt and pepper and toss well. Taste for seasoning and serve hot or at room temperature.

ROASTED PEPPERS WITH GARLIC

6 sweet bell peppers: red, yellow, green, orange, or purple
About 1/2 cup (120 ml) extra-virgin olive oil
6 cloves garlic, sliced thin lengthwise

About 12 fresh basil leaves or 4 Italian oregano sprigs 5 inches (13 cm) long
Salt and freshly ground pepper

Roast, peel, and seed the peppers. Cut them into sixths lengthwise.

Drizzle a little oil in the bottom of a shallow glass or ceramic baking dish. Arrange about one-third of the peppers in the the dish, scatter about one-third of the garlic and half the herbs over them, season lightly with salt and pepper, and drizzle with a little more oil. Repeat the layering with the remaining ingredients, ending with garlic and the remaining oil.

Cover the dish tightly with plastic wrap and let marinate at room temperature for 4 hours. The peppers can be made up to 8 hours in advance, but they should be refrigerated. Allow them to come to room temperature before serving.

When peppers are in season, these garlicky ones are a bright and delicious addition to any meal. Serve them as an appetizer with a crusty loaf of bread, some fresh mozzarella or smoked provolone, and a nice red wine, or as a vegetable accompaniment to grills and roasts, or as a salad course. Many variations of this dish are served all over Italy; sometimes capers or anchovies are added, but we like it best with just lots of garlic.

EGGPLANT SALAD WITH CHINESE-STYLE DRESSING

The cuisines of China's Hunan and Sichuan regions have many dishes in which garlic is essential. This is one of our favorites, rich with the flavors of garlic and oriental seasonings, yet light because the eggplant is steamed.

Dressing

3 tablespoons (45 ml) soy sauce
4 tablespoons (60 ml) rice wine vinegar
1 tablespoon (15 ml) white wine or dry sherry
4 tablespoons (60 ml) vegetable oil
2 tablespoons (30 ml) dark sesame oil

1/2 teaspoon (2 ml) hot red pepper oil, or to taste
4 or 5 garlic cloves, minced
1 green onion with some green, minced
2 teaspoons (10 ml) minced ginger

Prepare the dressing before you cook the eggplant. Place soy sauce, vinegar, and wine or sherry in a bowl. Whisk in the vegetable oil, sesame oil, and hot pepper oil, stir in the garlic, green onion, and ginger.

Salad

1½ pounds (675 g) long, thin eggplants
1/4 cup (60 ml) loosely packed

coriander leaves
2 or 3 green onions with some green, sliced thin

Trim the stems from the eggplants and steam the whole eggplants until they are tender, about 7 minutes. When they are cool enough to handle, cut them in half lengthwise, then crosswise into slices about 1/2 inch (1 cm) thick.

Toss the eggplant with the dressing and arrange on a serving platter. Scatter the coriander leaves and green onions over the salad and let it marinate at cool room temperature for an hour or so, or serve immediately.

Eggplant Salad with Chinese-Style Dressing

White Bean Salad

The blend of herbs and garlic gives this salad a Middle Eastern flavor. It makes a substantial lunch or a light dinner accompanied by pita bread and olives. Red, green, or yellow bell pepper strips or rings are a handsome and tasty garnish. Any white bean can be used, such as great northern, navy, or cannellini.

1 pound (450 g) white beans
1 teaspoon (5 ml) salt
1/4 cup (60 ml) extra-virgin olive oil
3 tablespoons (45 ml) lemon juice
4 or 5 garlic cloves, minced
1/3 cup (80 ml) minced parsley
1/4 cup (60 ml) snipped chives
2 tablespoons (30 ml) minced mint
Salt and freshly ground pepper
1 large tomato, diced

Soak the beans overnight, drain, and cover them by about an inch (2 cm) of fresh water. Cook the beans with the salt, stirring occasionally, until they are tender but firm: 45 to 60 minutes depending on their variety and age. Be sure that there is some liquid in the bottom of the pan throughout the cooking time. Drain the beans and reserve the cooking liquid for another use.

In a small bowl, combine the olive oil, lemon juice, garlic, parsley, chives, and mint. Season with salt and pepper and stir well. Place the beans in a large bowl, add the tomato, and pour the dressing over all. Toss well. Refrigerate the salad for at least an hour before serving so that the flavors have time to meld. Taste for seasoning.

Remove from refrigerator about 20 to 30 minutes before serving to serve at cool room temperature. Serve from the bowl or arrange on salad plates with lettuce and peppers, if desired.

CONDIMENTS AND ACCOMPANIMENTS

Garlic Pickles, Garlic Marinated Olives, and Kim Chi

Garlic Pickles

We cold-pack these pickles so that the cucumbers can be cooked in the boiling water bath and still remain crunchy. Not at all sweet, these tart and garlicky pickles are a fine munch with any sandwich. Small French pickling cucumbers, or cornichons, work well in this recipe.

Generous 3 pounds (1.4 kg) pickling cucumbers
3½ cups (830 ml) water
2½ cups (590 ml) cider vinegar
1 tablespoon (15 ml) dill seed
2 teaspoons (10 ml) yellow mustard seed

1 teaspoon (5 ml) peppercorns
1/3 cup (80 ml) pickling or kosher salt
3 bay leaves
36 garlic cloves, peeled and halved lengthwise

Scrub the cucumbers well. Have ready six sterilized canning jars with lids and rings.

In a noncorrodible pot, combine the water, vinegar, dill and mustard seed, peppercorns, salt, and bay leaves. Heat over medium heat until the mixture comes to a boil. Reduce heat and simmer 5 minutes.

Cut the cucumbers in quarters lengthwise or use whole cornichons. Pack the cucumbers into the jars and distribute the garlic evenly among the jars.

Remove the bay leaves from the pickling brine. Ladle the boiling liquid over the cucumbers, taking care to distribute the spices equally, and leaving 1/4 inch head space. Wipe the rims and screw on the lids and rings.

Process jars for 15 minutes in a boiling water bath according to manufacturer's instructions.

Remove the jars from the boiling water and let them cool to room temperature away from drafts. Store sealed jars in a cool place. If any jars do not seal, keep them in the refrigerator. The pickles will be ready to eat in 2 to 3 weeks.

GARLIC MARINATED OLIVES

Green olives

1 pound (450 g) plain brine-cured, cracked green olives, with brine
5 garlic cloves, smashed
1/4 cup (60 ml) white wine vinegar

2 or 3 short sprigs Italian or Greek oregano, optional
2 or 3 small, whole hot red chilis, optional

We've provided recipes for both cracked green olives or oil-cured black olives; it is nice to have both on hand. When buying the green olives, be sure they are covered with brine; the olives should account for about 8 ounces (225 g) of weight and the brine, the remainder.

Drain the olives and reserve the brine. Measure 2/3 cup (160 ml) of the brine and mix it with the vinegar. In a pint (1/2 litre) jar with a tight-fitting lid, layer the olives with the garlic, and the oregano and chilis, if you like.

Pour the brine mixture over the olives and close the jar. Marinate the olives in the refrigerator for at least 5 days before using. They will keep refrigerated for as long as 6 months.

Black olives

8 ounces (225 g) black oil-cured olives
5 garlic cloves, smashed
1/2 lemon, sliced thin

1/4 cup (60 ml) lemon juice
1/2 cup (120 ml) water
2 or 3 thyme sprigs, optional
Bay leaf, optional

Place a lemon slice in the bottom of a pint (1/2 litre) jar. Layer the olives, garlic, and remaining lemon, and the optional thyme or bay. Mix the lemon juice with the water and add just enough to cover the olives. Marinate the olives in the refrigerator for at least 5 days before using. They will keep refrigerated for as long as 6 months.

KIM CHI: KOREAN GARLIC PICKLED CABBAGE

Kim chi or kim chee is a condiment that Koreans serve with nearly every meal and always with rice. This is a potent food, appealing to those who like strong flavors and texture. We know non-Koreans who have become addicted to its very garlicky and very hot and spicy flavor. Many of its fans claim good health and longevity from eating it. During the pickling process, kim chi gives off strong odors that can affect the contents of the refrigerator.

2 pounds (900 g) Napa or
    Chinese cabbage
2 tablespoons (30 ml) kosher salt
2 teaspoons (10 ml) cayenne pepper
8 cups (2 litres) cold water
10 garlic cloves, minced, about 1/4
    cup (60 ml)
3 tablespoons (45 ml) minced fresh
    ginger root
2 or 3 fresh green or red chilis,
    minced

2 bunches green onions, trimmed with
    2 to 3 inches (5 to 8 cm) of
    green and cut crosswise into
    1/2-inch (1-cm) slices
1 to 2 tablespoons (15 to 30 ml)
    cayenne pepper, according to heat
    desired
1½ teaspoons (8 ml) kosher salt
1 teaspoon (5 ml) sugar
2 cups (475 ml) water

Cut the cabbage lengthwise into quarters. Cut it crosswise into slices about an inch (2 cm) wide. Place about half the cabbage in a large stainless steel bowl or ceramic crock. Sprinkle it with 1 tablespoon (15 ml) of the salt and 1 teaspoon (5 ml) of the cayenne. Add the rest of the cabbage and sprinkle with the remaining tablespoon (15 ml) of salt and teaspoon (5 ml) of cayenne.

Pour 8 cups (2 litres) of cold water over the cabbage. Press the cabbage down so that it is all moistened and place a plate and a weight on it to hold it down.

Place the cabbage in a cool place for 24 hours, stirring once and replacing the plate.

Drain the cabbage and rinse it well with cold water. Drain it again and squeeze out excess liquid.

Place the cabbage in a bowl and add the garlic, ginger, chilis, and scallions. Toss well. Add the remaining cayenne and salt and the sugar and toss well.

Pack the cabbage mixture into two sterile quart (1-litre) canning jars. Cover the cabbage with cold water, about 1 cup (240 ml) per jar, and use a chopstick to distribute the cabbage evenly and release any air bubbles.

Cover the jars with a double layer of waxed paper or cheesecloth and screw a canning ring on top. Place the jars in the refrigerator and leave them for 3 to 4 days.

Taste to see if the kim chi is "pickled" enough for your liking. If not, leave it for 2 or 3 days longer. Replace the waxed paper or cheesecloth, cover with a metal canning lid and ring, and keep the kim chi for as long as a month in the refrigerator.

GARLIC CHEESE SPREADS

Makes about 2 cups (475 ml)

Homemade cheese spreads are less expensive and offer many more variations than those commercially made. They can be, as are those below, lighter in texture and more flavorful, too. Experimenting with different herb combinations is not only fun, but adds interest even to low-fat and low-salt spreads. In addition to their uses as spreads, these cheese mixtures are also good as dips for crudités. They can be kept in the refrigerator, tightly covered, for as long as five days.

Basic Spread

1/2 pound (225 g) natural cream cheese, softened
1/2 cup (120 ml) sour cream
3 garlic cloves, minced

2 tablespoons (30 ml) minced parsley
Salt and freshly ground pepper
2 or 3 dashes angostura bitters

Combine the cream cheese with the sour cream in a small bowl. Add the garlic and parsley, blending well. Add the bitters and salt and pepper to taste. Cover the cheese tightly and refrigerate for at least 1 hour before serving.

Variations

Add a teaspoon (5 ml) herb vinegar for a tangier flavor.

Use whole milk or low-fat ricotta to replace all or part of the cream cheese.

Substitute 4 ounces (115 g) fresh mild goat cheese or feta for half the cream cheese.

Add a tablespoon (15 ml) or so of minced basil, dill, or tarragon, or a teaspoon (5 ml) or so of minced rosemary, sage, or thyme.

ROASTED GARLIC

Roasting separate cloves

1 head garlic
1/2 cup (120 ml) olive oil
2 or 3 thyme sprigs

1 bay leaf
Salt and freshly ground pepper

Preheat the oven to 250°F (120°C). Break the garlic head into cloves, leaving the inner skins on. Place the garlic in a small oven-proof dish and add the olive oil, thyme, and bay leaf. Season lightly with salt and pepper.

Bake the garlic until it is very tender, about 40 minutes. Turn the cloves over from time to time. Remove the dish from the oven and let the garlic cool to room temperature.

Roasting garlic on the grill

For each head of garlic you will need:

Aluminum foil
About 1/2 tablespoon (8 ml) olive oil
Salt and freshly ground pepper

2 or 3 thyme sprigs, optional
1 bay leaf, optional

For the grill, remove the outer layers of garlic skin. Slice off about 1/2 inch (1 cm) of the stem to expose the cloves slightly.

Cut enough foil to triple regular foil, or double heavy-duty foil for each head of garlic. Place it on the foil cut side up, and mold the foil to it, leaving the cut top exposed. Drizzle with olive oil, season with salt and pepper, and add herbs, if desired. If you're grilling with the lid on, leave the package open to absorb the

There are several ways to roast garlic, each with its advantages. Roasting on the grill is handy when you have a grilled menu. Whole heads or half heads may also be roasted in the oven; there is even a terra-cotta garlic roaster made for this purpose. Roasting separate cloves is best when you will be incorporating them in another dish, such as Garlic Soufflé (page 28) or Mashed Potatoes (page 53). Whichever technique you choose will result in fragrant, nutty-sweet garlic to enhance grilled foods, rustic breads, pizzas and foccacias, as well as pastas, particularly those with chicken or cream sauces.

smoky flavor. If you're grilling without a lid, crimp the foil closed so the package can be turned.

Roast the garlic over a medium-low fire for about 30 minutes; it should feel soft when pressed with tongs, or with your fingers protected by an oven mitt.

Remove garlic from the fire and unwrap. Serve warm or at room temperature.

Roasting garlic in the oven

Assemble same ingredients as for roasting on the grill. Preheat the oven to 300°F (150°C). Remove the outer layers of garlic skin. Leave the heads whole, cut them in half crosswise, or slice off about 1/2 inch (1 cm) of the stem to expose the cloves slightly.

Cut enough foil to triple regular foil, or double heavy-duty foil for each head or half head. Place the garlic on the foil cut side up, drizzle with olive oil, season with salt and pepper, and add herbs, if desired. Wrap the package tightly.

Roast the garlic for 30 minutes, or until it gives when pressed. Unwrap it and serve it warm or at room temperature.

DESSERTS

Chocolate-Covered Garlic

Chocolate-Covered Garlic

Chocolate-covered garlic bonbons are for those with adventurous palates and a passion for garlic in any form. Light red wines such as merlot or chianti work well in this recipe, but whatever decent red wine you have on hand could be used instead. At Chez Panisse restaurant in Berkeley, California, the pastry chefs have poached fresh figs in a similar mixture of wine, garlic, and sugar. We have specified the brand of chocolate, as some do not melt well and make rather lumpy-looking bonbons.

24 medium-sized garlic cloves
1/2 cup (120 ml) red wine
1/4 cup (60 ml) sugar
2-inch (5 cm) piece of lemon rind,
    yellow part only

2 ounces (60 g) bittersweet or
    semisweet Lindt or Baker's
    chocolate

Peel the garlic cloves and remove the root end. Discard any cloves that have brown spots or cut them away.

Bring the garlic, wine, sugar, and lemon rind to a simmer in a small, heavy noncorrodible saucepan. Reduce the heat, cover, and cook over low heat for 25 to 30 minutes, stirring occasionally. Test the garlic for tenderness with the point of a sharp knife.

Cool the garlic cloves on a plate covered with a piece of waxed paper. They will be very sticky.

Melt the chocolate in a double boiler over medium heat. Cover another plate with a piece of waxed paper.

Stick a toothpick in a clove of garlic. Hold it over the edge of the pan, and with a small spoon, cover the clove lightly with the melted chocolate. Place the coated clove on the waxed paper to cool and harden. Coat the remaining cloves.

Store the chocolate-covered cloves in a covered container in a cool place. Do not refrigerate or the chocolate will change color. These are best eaten within 24 to 48 hours.

GARLIC HONEY ICE CREAM

6 large garlic cloves, peeled
2/3 cup or 8 ounces (160 ml or
  225 g) light honey such as orange
  or clover
1 cup (240 ml) whipping (double)
  cream

2 cups (475 ml) half-and-half
  (single) cream
3 egg yolks

Garlic and honey are an ancient combination used in various cultures to treat colds and coughs and as a general tonic. Here, we heat the ingredients together to infuse the honey with garlic flavor, but traditionally peeled garlic cloves are simply steeped in honey for a week or longer. Honey is hygroscopic, drawing out garlic's moisture and flavor. Most people who eat this ice cream cannot identify garlic in it, though they can tell that it contains some unusual ingredient. The honey gives a fine texture.

Place the garlic and honey in a small heavy saucepan. Bring the honey just to a simmer over low heat. This takes about 5 minutes, but watch carefully, as the honey can bubble over and/or caramelize all at once. Remove the pan from heat, cover, and let the garlic steep overnight. Remove the garlic when you are ready to proceed.

Dissolve the honey in the creams over medium-low heat. Beat the egg yolks lightly in a small bowl. Beat in about a half cup (120 ml) of cream to warm the egg yolks, then pour the yolk mixture to the pan. Stir the mixture over medium low heat until the custard just coats a metal spoon.

Strain the custard through a sieve into a bowl and chill it thoroughly, covered, overnight in the refrigerator or in an ice water bath.

Pour the chilled custard into an ice cream freezer and follow the manufacturer's instructions.

BIBLIOGRAPHY

BOOKS

Batcheller, Barbara. *Lilies of the Kitchen.* New York: St. Martin's Press, 1986.

Crawford, Stanley. *A Garlic Testament: Seasons on a Small New Mexico Farm.* New York: Harper Collins, 1992.

Creasy, Rosalind. *Cooking from the Garden.* San Francisco: Sierra Club Books, 1988.

Dille, Carolyn, and Susan Belsinger. *Herbs in the Kitchen: A Celebration of Flavor.* Loveland, Colorado: Interweave Press, 1992.

Forbes, Leslie. *A Taste of Tuscany.* Boston: Little, Brown, 1985.

Foster, Gertrude, and Rosemary Louden. *Park's Success with Herbs.* Greenwood, South Carolina: George W. Park Seed Company, 1980.

Garland, Sarah. *The Complete Book of Herbs and Spices.* New York: Viking, 1979.

Grieve, M. *A Modern Herbal.* New York: Dover, 1971.

Hale, Sophie. *The Great Garlic Cookbook.* London: Quintent, 1986.

Harris, Lloyd John. *The Book of Garlic.* Berkeley: Aris Books, 1974.

————, and Rose Harris. *The Official Garlic Lover's Handbook.* Berkeley: Aris Books, 1986.

Mazza, Irma Goodrich. *Herbs for the Kitchen.* Boston: Little, Brown, 1975.

Miloradovich, Milo. *Growing and Using Herbs and Spices.* New York: Dover, 1952.

Rodale, Robert, editor. *How to Grow Vegetables and Fruits by the Organic Method.* Emmaus, Pennsylvania: Rodale Books, 1973.

Romer, Elizabeth. *The Tuscan Year: Life and Food in an Italian Valley.* New York: Atheneum, 1985.

Schuler, Stanley, editor. *Simon and Schuster's Guide to Herbs and Spices.* New York: Fireside Books, 1990.

Simmons, Adelma Grenier. *Herb Gardening in Five Seasons.* New York: Hawthorn, 1964.

Stobart, Tom. *Herbs, Spices, and Flavorings.* New York: Overlook Press, 1982.

Toklas, Alice B. *The Alice B. Toklas Cook Book.* New York: Harper & Row, 1984.

Waters, Alice. *The Chez Panisse Menu Cookbook.* New York: Random House, 1982.

PERIODICALS

Dille, Carolyn. "Garlic: A Cook's Notes." *The Herb Companion,* August/September 1990, pp. 18–24.

Fackelmann, Kathy A. "Nursing babes savor garlic, shun spirits." *Science News,* October 12, 1991, p. 230.

Health Letter Associates. "Garlic, the food-aceutical." The University of California, *Berkeley Wellness Letter,* March 1992, p. 1.

Martin, Dennis. "Folklore, old wives were right: garlic stimulates the immune system, fights free radicals, inhibits tumors." *Health News & Review,* December 1991, p. 1.

Marwick, Charles "And some recommend it as a vampire prophylactic." *Journal of the American Medical Association,* November 28, 1990, p. 2614.

Sanchez, Janet. "Growing and Harvesting Garlic." *Horticulture,* October 1992, pp. 52–3.

Yee, Sandra Y. "Why Garlic is good for you." *McCall's,* November 1991, p. 20.

FILMS

Blank, Les. *Garlic is as Good as Ten Mothers.* El Cerrito, California: Flower Films, 1980.